Ming

art, people and places

Ming

art, people and places

Jessica Harrison-Hall

The British Museum

© 2014 The Trustees of the British Museum

Jessica Harrison-Hall has asserted the right to
be identified as the author of this work.

First published in 2014 by The British Museum Press
A division of The British Museum Company Ltd
38 Russell Square, London WC1B 3QQ
britishmuseum.org/publishing

A catalogue reference for this book is available
from the British Library

ISBN 978 0 7141 2483 4

Designed by Raymonde Watkins
Printed and bound in Italy by Rotolito Lombarda Spa

Half title page: Inlaid lacquer tray with scene
showing two riders in a landscape with
an attendant; 1500–1600; h 18.6 cm, w 18.6 cm;
British Museum.
Title page: *Cloisonné* jar and cover; Xuande mark
and period, 1426–35; h 62 cm, w 55.9 cm;
British Museum.
Opposite: Blue-and-white porcelain flask;
Yongle period, 1403–24; h 30.8 cm;
Sir Percival David Collection.

Contents

Introduction

The Ming dynasty was a golden age and has a particular resonance in Europe as it marks the moment when direct trading relations were established firstly through the Portuguese and Spanish and latterly by the Dutch and English. As a result of this contact, bulk export of Ming blue-and-white porcelains transformed interiors and dining habits in the West. However, for Ming China this interaction was just one small part of its intricate trading and diplomatic relationships with foreign countries. The focus was not on Europe but on the neighbouring countries in Asia, the Middle East and even Africa. Today the Ming are remembered for their monuments: they established the capital in Beijing with the Forbidden City at its heart and reconstructed the Great Wall of China as we see it today.

Ming 明 means 'brilliant', combining the characters for the sun 日 and the moon 月. Traditionally it has been regarded as a beacon of Han Chinese rule between the Mongol Yuan dynasty (1279–1368) and the Manchu Qing dynasty (1644–1911). Along with the Han (206 BC–AD 220) and Tang (AD 618–906) dynasties, it is hailed as an era that defines national Chinese identity, but this identity is multi-faceted and incorporates many external influences. Ming is hard to regard as a single entity because Ming China is so very different in the late 1300s to the early 1600s. The population, economy and territory all expanded significantly.

Ming China was a gloriously complicated place and turning 276 years of stories into a simple short narrative is a challenging task. Through a selection of paintings, texts and objects that survive from the period, this book opens a window onto the imperial palaces, the outdoor spaces enjoyed by the elite, the production centres for luxury goods, the tombs that have yielded some spectacular finds, and the religious beliefs of Ming China's vast population.

The Great Wall of China is today a powerful symbol of China. It was much restored during the Ming dynasty and if you look closely it is easy to find bricks marked with Ming production dates.

Reign title	Reign period	Family Name	Temple Name
Hongwu 洪武	1368–1398	Zhu Yuanzhang 朱元璋	Taizu 太祖
Jianwen 建文	1399–1402	Zhu Yunwen 朱允炆	Huidi 惠帝
Yongle 永樂	1403–1424	Zhu Di 朱棣	Chengzu 成祖 or Taizong 太宗
Hongxi 洪熙	1425	Zhu Gaozhi 朱高熾	Renzong 仁宗
Xuande 宣德	1426–1435	Zhu Zhanji 朱瞻基	Xuanzong 宣宗
Zhengtong 正統	1436–1449	Zhu Qizhen 朱祁鎮	Yingzong 英宗
Jingtai 景泰	1450–1456	Zhu Qiyu 朱祁鈺	Daizong 代宗
Tianshun 天順	1457–1464	Zhu Qizhen 朱祁鎮	Yingzong 英宗
Chenghua 成化	1465–1487	Zhu Jianshen 朱見深	Xianzong 憲宗
Hongzhi 弘治	1488–1505	Zhu Youtang 朱祐樘	Xiaozong 孝宗
Zhengde 正德	1506–1521	Zhu Haozhao 朱厚照	Wuzong 武宗
Jiajing 嘉靖	1522–1566	Zhu Houcong 朱厚熜	Shizong 世宗
Longqing 隆慶	1567–1572	Zhu Zaihou 朱載坖	Muzong 穆宗
Wanli 萬曆	1573–1619	Zhu Yijun 朱翊鈞	Shenzong 神宗
Taichang 泰昌	1620	Zhu Changluo 朱常洛	Guangzong 光宗
Tianqi 天啟	1621–1627	Zhu Youxiao 朱由校	Xizong 熹宗
Chongzhen 崇禎	1628–1644	Zhu Youjian 朱由檢	Sizong 思宗

**Robe belonging to Zhu Tan,
Prince Huang of Lu**
Silk
1380–9
China
h 125 cm, w 218 cm
Shandong Museum

1

Palaces and the Ming imperial family

The imperial family

A succession of sixteen emperors ruled China during the Ming dynasty (1368–1644), with one ruling twice. These hereditary rulers governed for 276 years, spanning a period that in English history would stretch from the publication of Geoffrey Chaucer's *Canterbury Tales* to the Civil War between the Roundheads and the Cavaliers. Remarkably, after the Hongwu emperor (r. 1368–1398) founded the dynasty, the throne generally passed directly from father to son. The main succession was interrupted only twice: once by force, when the Yongle emperor (r. 1403–1424) seized the throne from his nephew; and once by design, when the Jiajing emperor (r. 1522–1566) was invited to take power as his predecessor, the Zhengde emperor (r. 1505–1521), had no male heirs.

Anonymous, 'Portrait of the Yongle emperor'
Hanging scroll, ink and colours on silk
c. 1424
Beijing
h 220 cm, w 150 cm
National Palace Museum

The first Ming emperor, Hongwu, had a meteoric rise to power. He was a priest, then a soldier, becoming Son of Heaven by the age of forty. He defeated the Mongol Yuan dynasty and drove its leaders to the northern and southern borders of the empire. Consequently, his domestic and foreign policies centred on recovery from the long years of war. Perhaps his varied roles before becoming emperor helped him to understand the plight of his people and their need for stability. He reconstructed farms, forests and infrastructure. He also established a fabulous new capital in the city of Nanjing, which was close to fertile rice-growing lands and the Yangtze river for transportation.

Empress Ma (1332–1382) was his principal wife. Imperial wives were chosen from a broad social pool to avoid opposition to the throne from noble families. Through multiple wives of differing status, the Hongwu emperor had twenty-six sons and sixteen daughters. Very few images of imperial Ming women survive, but an album compiled during the dynasty records the different Ming emperors, their main wives and their mothers in bust portraits, dressed in formal costume and crowns.

CHAPTER OPENER
**Anonymous, 'Portrait of
the Hongwu emperor'**
Hanging scroll, ink and
colours on silk
c. 1400
Nanjing
h 268.8 cm, w 163.8 cm
National Palace Museum

LEFT
**Anonymous, 'Portrait of
the Jiajing emperor'**
Hanging scroll, ink and
colours on silk
c. 1566
Beijing
h 209.7 cm, w 155.2 cm
National Palace Museum

FOLLLOWING PAGES
**Anonymous,
'Portrait of the Hongxi
emperor and his wife'**
Album leaf, ink and
colours on silk
c. 1425
Beijing
With mount: h 83.4 cm,
w 123.2 cm
National Palace Museum

天明仁宗昭皇帝

Princes and their wives

To protect the borders, rivers and land of the new empire, the Hongwu emperor sent his sons to fiefdoms across the country to represent imperial power in the regions. Ming China was a state the size of a continent and each of these princes symbolized imperial power in regions the size of modern European countries. For example, the Princes of Shu represented the emperor in Sichuan, which is the same size as modern France. Some principalities were more than a thousand miles from the capital city and would have required months of overland travel to reach.

The princes' palaces had up to perhaps 800 halls to accommodate their extensive families and a vast staff including servants of all kinds, as well as eunuchs and religious, civil and military officials. We can only now understand the wealth and grandeur of these regional courts by piecing together references to them in contemporary texts and by examining the discoveries of archaeologists over the past fifty years.

Group of figures from
the tomb of Prince
Huang of Lu, Zhu Tan
Pinewood, traces of paint,
silk, bronze
c. 1389
Shandong
Horse: h 31.7 cm,
w 30.9 cm
Shandong Museum

Emperors

The Hongwu emperor's eldest son died before him and so he was succeeded by his grandson, who became the Jianwen emperor (1399–1402). The Jianwen emperor's reign was blighted by a bitter civil war initiated by his uncle, one of the regional princes, who later became the Yongle emperor. The Jianwen emperor's palace at Nanjing was attacked and torched; Jianwen was killed and his body was never found.

The Yongle emperor was the fourth son of the Hongwu emperor. A skilled military strategist like his father, he led his own troops into battle. He gradually moved the capital to Beijing, where he had his palace as regional Prince of Yan on the site of the old Yuan capital city. Having usurped the throne, he focused his efforts on legitimizing his position and emphasizing his close relationship with his father, the Ming founder. As well as relocating the capital from Nanjing to Beijing and constructing the Forbidden City, he built up strong relationships with China's neighbours through tribute trade and diplomatic visits. He also commissioned six of the seven sea voyages undertaken by official armadas, including those commanded by his loyal eunuch Admiral Zheng He (1371–1433). These fleets successfully navigated the oceans to visit courts from Brunei to Mogadishu, extending a network of foreign contacts for the courts.

Unlike his father, the Yongle emperor, or his grandfather, the Hongwu emperor, the Hongxi emperor (r. 1424–1425) was not a skilled military tactician and preferred civil administration. Had he lived longer, he would have made Nanjing the main capital as there was still opposition to relocating the centre of power to the north.

The Xuande emperor (r. 1426–1435) led his troops into battle, putting down a domestic rebellion started by one of his uncles as well as keeping Mongol leaders at bay. In line with the ideal qualities of the day, the Xuande emperor was also respected for his administrative abilities and artistic talents. Some of his paintings survive and are among the finest by any emperor of China. Foreign policies established by his grandfather were continued and the last of Zheng He's voyages took place in his reign.

The Zhengtong emperor (r. 1436–1449 and 1457–1464) was the only emperor to rule twice. He ascended the throne as an eight-year-old child. In 1449, as a young man, he was captured while leading his troops against the

Scholars and servants waiting with their horses outside the Forbidden City. Anonymous, 'Painting of the Forbidden City' (detail) Handscroll, ink and colours on silk
c. 1480–1580
Beijing
h 204 cm, w 114 cm
British Museum

Mongols and held to ransom. At a moment of crisis for the dynasty, in his absence, his half-brother (1450–1457) was enthroned as the Jingtai emperor. After a year, the Mongols released the Zhengtong emperor but he had to wait for seven more years before he returned to the throne.

After the mid-fifteenth century, no other Ming emperor led his own troops into battle and there was a gradual shift from a court dominated by military culture to one in which civil officials had the upper hand. The relationships between the central and regional courts also changed. In the early fifteenth century, the rulers of the regional courts were initially sons of the emperor. Later, they were brothers or uncles or increasingly remote cousins of the emperor. As time progressed, these direct relationships were diluted, fewer audiences with the emperor were held and the number of regional courts increased, lessening the close personal family ties between the central imperial court and the regional princely courts. After the Yongle emperor, their military power also declined.

Paintings depicting life at court show the succeeding Chenghua emperor (r. 1465–1487), eunuchs, women and children enjoying firework displays, watching acrobats fly through hoops and listening to musicians. Lavish gold and silver vessels were used for eating and drinking. Large princely estates increased in size and urban populations grew. Centres for patronage developed outside the courts. Consequently the scale of manufacture and distribution of luxury goods increased.

The Chenghua emperor had only one surviving son, who became the Hongzhi emperor (r. 1488–1505). His son, the Zhengde emperor (r. 1506–1521), enjoyed dressing up and leaving the imperial palace compound to go about his people in disguise. He had a fascination for foreign scripts and studied some foreign languages. During his reign, Portuguese merchants began direct trade with China, bringing Chinese goods directly to Europe and in greater quantities.

A new line of the Ming imperial family was started by the Jiajing emperor (r. 1522–1566). He had been invited to take power as the Zhengde emperor died without a male heir. However, he provoked a constitutional crisis by honouring his birth parents with imperial tombs and refusing to accept his adopted father, the Zhengde emperor, as his real parent. The Jiajing emperor is celebrated for his Daoist beliefs and for surviving an assassination attempt

Anonymous, 'Portrait of the Wanli emperor's wife, Empress Xiaoduanxian, Wang Xijie'
Album leaf, ink and colours on silk
c. 1620
Beijing
h 65 cm, w 51.4 cm
National Palace Museum

Anonymous, 'Portrait of the Wanli emperor's wife, Imperial Noble Consort Wenshu'
Album leaf, ink and colours on silk
c. 1620
Beijing
h 64.9 cm, w 51.5 cm
National Palace Museum

by his concubines. During his reign, direct contact with Europe increased, and the middle classes in China flourished.

Although he only reigned for five years and died aged thirty-four, the Longqing emperor's reign (r. 1567–1572) saw the control of coastal pirates and the negotiation of peace with Mongol leaders.

The Wanli emperor (r. 1573–1619) ascended the throne at the age of ten and ruled for forty-seven years. He was buried with two wives in his elaborate tomb, the only Ming imperial tomb to have been excavated by archaeologists. During his reign, the population grew significantly as production of food increased. Cash crops and luxury goods brought new wealth and a growing middle class. This stimulated increased intellectual activity as well as a building boom and trade in the accoutrements of wealth. During the Wanli emperor's reign, the Jesuit priest Matteo Ricci (1552–1616) was recorded as the first European to enter the Forbidden City. Spanish and Portuguese merchants, later joined by the Dutch and English

**Anonymous,
'Portrait of the
Wanli emperor'**
Album leaf, ink and
colours on silk
c. 1573–1620
Beijing
h 65.1 cm,
w 51.4 cm
National Palace
Museum

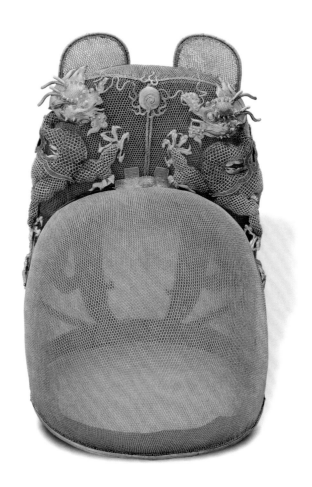

East India Companies, competed for direct trade with China, bringing
blue-and-white porcelain to the homes of the middle classes of Europe.
The Wanli emperor paid great attention to the construction of his tomb,
which was built like an underground palace. It was filled with real treasures,
including a gold crown for the emperor and an ornate gold, pearl and feather
crown for the empress. The Taichang emperor (r. 1620) ruled for only one
month and it was popularly believed that he was poisoned. He was followed
by the Tianqi emperor (r. 1621–1627), who was weak and possibly illiterate.

The Chongzhen emperor (r. 1628–1644) was the last of the seventeen Ming emperors. He committed suicide as his palace was invaded by northern Qing troops from Manchuria. He ordered the palace women to kill themselves and executed his own daughter and concubines to save them from the conquerors. After nearly three hundred years, this was the end of the official Ming dynasty, although a Southern Ming dynasty with claimants to the throne survived well into the Kangxi era (1662–1722).

The Wanli empress's crown
Gold, pearls, kingfisher feathers, coral
c. 1573–1619
Beijing
h 35.5 cm, w 20 cm
Dingling Museum, Beijing

2

Parks and gardens

the courts and officials

The lives of the Ming emperors are well documented in official histories and biographies. However, little is known of the peasant labourers who formed the greater part of Ming China's population. These people had few possessions and their burials contained no lavish tomb goods that we could now use to reconstruct their everyday existence. As they were illiterate, they left no written record of their lives, but a few personal details do appear in official documents such as household registers that record every citizen's name, home town, gender, age, address, profession and property.

The image above is from one of the earliest illustrated children's books and shows a land-worker dressed in a cape made from woven plants. It is labelled with the Chinese character meaning farmer. Pictures of ordinary labourers are very rare, although they do exist in certain genres of Ming painting such as religious art and in scenes of tilling and weaving. In monochrome Ming ink paintings, people are rarely depicted working on the land, unless they are posing as historical figures or are scholars who have withdrawn from society.

Aristocrats' parks and gardens

In the early Ming dynasty, some of the most famous and admired gardens belonged to the imperial aristocracy and military and civil leaders. Locations of aristocrat-owned gardens in the two Ming capitals, Beijing and Nanjing, can be established, but no trace of these gardens remains today.

Ming gardens were constructed with artificial and natural hills and lakes, waterways, buildings, and rocks worn through with natural holes. These spaces were enhanced with poetic inscriptions and plants that evoked literary allusions. Most Ming gardens sought to condense the natural world, compressing the essence of whole landscapes into a compact space. Even more distilled are the miniature gardens and plants that were grown in pots (*penzai*). Purple, lavender, sky blue and jade green glazed pots were made at Juntai in Henan province for the newly built Forbidden City and its gardens. These could be moved around the palace gardens and halls to create 'natural' scenes in even smaller enclosed spaces, including studies and altars.

'Official Jun' flowerpot, of the type depicted in the handscroll scene on p. 27
Glazed stoneware with gold lacquer repair
c. 1400–35
Yuxian, Henan province
h 19.7 cm
British Museum

Detail of the emperor playing golf from 'Amusements in the Xuande Emperor's Palace', Anonymous
Handscroll, ink and colours on silk
1426–1487
Beijing
Image: h 36.6 cm, l 687cm
The Palace Museum

Imperial sports and entertainment

Within the palace gardens, the emperors and their court practised a number of sports, including archery, polo and early forms of football and golf. Such games have a long history in China and were not only played by the palace eunuchs and elite male troops that surrounded the emperor but also by palace ladies. Du Jin (active 1465–1509), who was not a court artist, painted palace ladies playing a form of golf (*chuiwan*). Judging by their costumes, these ladies probably represent figures from ancient history rather than contemporary Ming palace ladies.

The court was entertained with firework displays in the imperial gardens, including rockets and firecrackers. At festivals such as the lantern festival, lanterns were carried and displayed in a great variety of forms, including elephant-shaped lanterns. Within gardens, plays were staged, musical entertainments conducted, and stilt-walkers and acrobats performed.

BELOW LEFT
Du Jin (active 1465–1509),
'Court Ladies in the Inner
Palace'
Handscroll, ink and colours
on silk
c. 1465–1509
China
h 30.5 cm
Shanghai Museum

BELOW RIGHT
Detail of children in the
palace gardens from
'Lantern Festival Celebrated
in Emperor Xianzong
(Chenghua)'s Palace'
Handscroll, ink and colours
on silk
Dated 1485
Beijing
h 37 cm, l 624 cm
National Museum of China

ABOVE
**Lü Ji (c. 1429–c. 1505), fan
painted with a bird on a
hibiscus branch**
Ink and colours on paper
c. 1487–1505
Beijing
h 17.9 cm, w 44.3 cm
National Palace Museum

RIGHT
Garden seats
Porcelain with polychrome glazes
c. 1488–1566
Jingdezhen, Jiangxi province
h 41.6 cm; 38.4 cm; 36.5 cm
British Museum and Sir Percival
David Collection

Garden furnishings

During the Ming dynasty, ceramic garden furniture developed, including vast porcelain tanks for rearing exotic fish and growing water plants such as lilies. Barrel-shaped garden seats were made in porcelain at Jingdezhen. These are heavily potted and covered in bright glazes, which meant they could be left outside in all weathers. Fans became popular in China after they were imported from Korea or Japan in large numbers in the fifteenth century. They were a prerequisite of summer.

Imperial hunting grounds and zoos

The Ming emperors kept large parks filled with deer, hare, rabbits and birds for hunting excursions. These riding trips were a good way for the Ming emperors to bond with their officials and to keep the military fit for battles, in which the cavalry played a major role.

From the days of the earliest imperial parks, exotic animals were a feature of an emperor's garden. The Yongle emperor was presented with a giraffe from the Sultan of Bengal in September 1414 (see overleaf). He was later presented with other giraffes and also kept elephants, zebras, lions, monkeys and birds, including peacocks. Similarly his great grand-son, the Chenghua emperor, was given a lioness and the event was recorded in a painting (see overleaf). The calligraphy above the painting is a rhapsody on the lioness written by the Chenghua Emperor. In the late Ming, the imperial gardens were visited by the well-to-do. Shen Defu, a writer and bureaucrat, recorded visits to the Western Park, the principal palace gardens in Beijing, where chickens and dogs were thrown to tigers and leopards in the menagerie to feed them.

Shang Xi (fl. 1426–35),
'The Xuande emperor on
an outing' (detail)
Hanging scroll, ink and colours
on paper
1426–35
Beijing
h 211 cm, w 353 cm
The Palace Museum

**Anonymous, calligraphy
by Shen Du (1357–1434),
'Tribute giraffe from Bengal'
(detail)**
Hanging scroll, ink and colours
on silk
*c.*1414
Nanjing or Beijing
h 90.4 cm, w 45 cm
National Palace Museum

OPPOSITE
**Anonymous,
detail of a 'Lioness'**
Handscroll, ink and colours
on paper
Dated 1483
China
Image h 242 cm, w 287 cm;
with mount: h 315, w 314 cm
Private Collection

Scholars' gardens

There was already a vast body of literature describing and praising famous gardens, but in the early 1630s Ji Cheng published *The Craft of Gardens* (*Yuan Yě*), the first book that included the technical processes and theories behind building and shaping a garden. Its focus was on the areas surrounding the modern cities of Shanghai, Nanjing, Hangzhou and Suzhou. The Humble Administrator's Garden, *Zhuo zheng yuan*, is the largest surviving private garden in Suzhou. It is based on a Ming garden once painted by the famous artist Wen Zhengming (1470–1559). It has distinctive white-washed walls, grey tiles and dark wood.

Private gardens were created in the busy cities for the wealthy to enjoy the illusion of space – mountains and forests, the freshness of running water and lakes. They were places to entertain friends and family in an elegant and fashionable style. From contemporary Ming paintings, we can see how these gatherings were conducted with food, wine, music and an airing of antiques, collectables and paintings. Indoor activities could easily be taken outside to a garden setting, as demonstrated by the picture above showing children sitting on a mat doing calligraphy.

草堂詩為
丁君潛德賦并畫

Outings and picnics

ABOVE
**Tang Yin (1470–1523),
'Thatched cottage in the
Western Mountain'**
Handscroll, ink and
colours on paper
c. 1490–1523
Jiangsu Province
Image: h 31.2 cm, l 146.3
cm; with mount: h 32 cm,
l 876.8 cm
British Museum

The handscroll above shows a scholar (far right), who is living in the countryside, far from the capital, surrounded by beautiful mountains and lakes. The detail of a blue-and-white jar (below) depicts officials riding on horseback to visit friends in the countryside. Two servants carry a sword and a zither (a musical string instrument), and two at the rear shoulder stacking lacquer picnic boxes and lidded jars of wine.

In addition to visual evidence, texts describing various foods survive. *Important Principles of Correct Diet (Yin Shan Zheng Yao)* was written in *c.* 1330 by Hu Sihui and was reprinted in 1456 with an imperial preface by the Jingtai emperor. This illustrated book about food and drink recorded recipes of

Chinese and non-Chinese dishes and also contained information about two hundred different kinds of medicinal herbs. It explained, too, how illness could be caused if someone's diet was deficient in certain foods.

Wealthy people of the Ming dynasty enjoyed outdoor spaces and made the most of their environment. As Ji Cheng wrote in *The Craft of Gardens*, 'There is no definite way of making the most of scenery; you know it is right when it stirs your emotions'. In the case of the emperors and the imperial court, they amused themselves in the palace gardens, kept exotic menageries and enjoyed hunting in open parks. Scholars made the most of smaller spaces and incorporated the natural world in their gardens.

BELOW
Detail of a scene painted on a wine jar showing three horseman and their servants on a picnic
Porcelain with underglaze cobalt-blue decoration
c. 1454–67
Jingdezhen, Jiangxi province
h 34 cm, w 36 cm
British Museum

3

Ming luxury goods

their producers and consumers

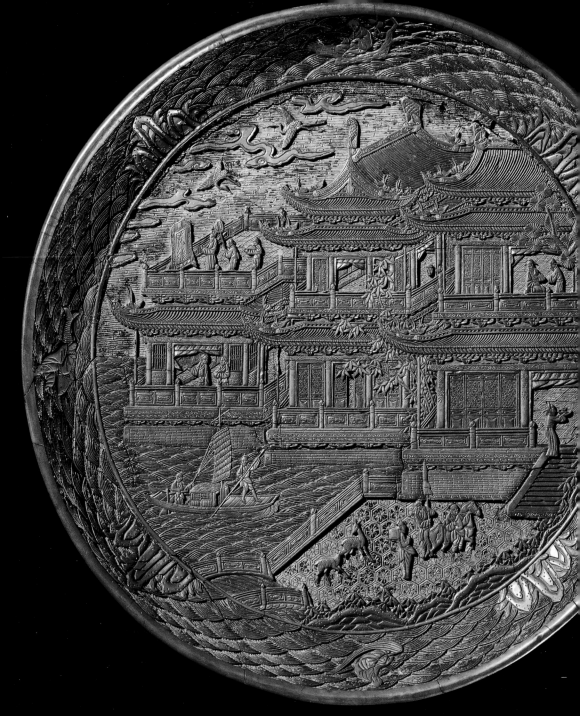

In the early Ming period, a number of luxury goods were made within the imperial palace compound itself and its environs, including *cloisonné*, gold and silver vessels, some jewellery with precious and semi-precious gems, and lacquer wares. Other luxury goods, such as porcelain and textiles, were produced further afield. The imperial courts imported luxury goods from across the Ming empire and consumed luxury goods that had been presented as tribute. Imperial palace buildings in Nanjing and Beijing required furnishings of the finest quality. The emperors also presented exquisite goods to other courts across Eurasia.

Cloisonné

Cloisonné-decorated vessels are not found in tombs or export contexts. Artisans made them in a eunuch-supervised office within the imperial court for palace halls and temples. *Cloisonné*-decorated vessels were made by applying melted

CHAPTER OPENER
Lacquer dish with inscription
Polychrome lacquer on wood core
Dated 1489
Maker from Gansu province
diam. 19 cm
British Museum

Cloisonné **box with lotus**
Enamels on bronze, gilding
c. 1400–50
Probably Beijing
h 8 cm, diam. 15.6 cm
British Museum

glass pastes into a design formed of wire cells attached to a metal body such as a vase, jar, dish or box. These vessels were then heated at a temperature high enough to fire the glass but not too high to melt the metal core and wires. The glass shrank on cooling, so sometimes this process had to be repeated several times to fill the cell. At first, a palette dominated by red, yellow, and ink-blue was used but gradually more colours were introduced. Eventually, several different colours were used within a single cell, creating more elaborate designs, including figures and landscapes.

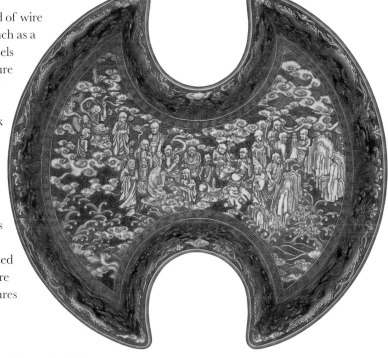

Lacquer

Lacquer is the sap collected from the trunk of the Chinese lacquer tree (*Toxicodendron verniciﬂuum*). The raw sap is toxic and contact with it can cause extreme dermatitis. The sap is filtered and heat-treated, then applied with a brush in layers onto a wooden core covered with textile. Red lacquer is coloured with cinnabar, a common ore of the mineral mercury.

Each layer of varnish took up to twenty-four hours to harden and dry before the next layer could be applied. A carved red lacquer object such as the dish pictured above has up to a hundred layers of lacquer. After carving, the edges of the design were polished using a powder, possibly of bone, horn or clay. In the early Ming, lacquer was deeply carved to create sculpted designs. Some of the finest pieces from this time show scenes with figures and fine architecture. The lacquer dish pictured on the chapter opener is unusual as it is signed by its maker and dated 'Carved by Wang Ming of Pingliang in the second year of the Hongzhi reign (1489)' (弘治二年平涼王銘刁).

Ingot-shaped
lacquer dish
Cinnabar coloured
lacquer on wood core
Jiajing mark and period,
1522–66
China
h 5.4 cm, diam. 32.8 cm
British Museum

Silver and gold

The imperial family used silver and gold vessels. These were made in a department of the imperial household that specialized in gold and silver working, which was called the *Yinzuoju* (The Jewellery Service). Many gold vessels were melted down by later generations, as their forms fell out of fashion. Other gold vessels may have been buried in tombs that have not yet been discovered. Gold workers at the imperial court incised this flask (left) with an imperial dragon pattern. The modelling of the vessel, particularly the cover and the method of fitting it, relates closely to the ewers found by archaeologists in the tomb of Prince Zhuang of Liang (1411–1441), dated 1424. The shape of the flask ultimately derives from Middle Eastern metalwork and was also reproduced in porcelain, but no porcelain covers for such flasks of this period survive, if they were ever made. Servants presented food to the emperor in gold dishes and bowls. Drinks were served separately, as depicted in the scene from a handscroll painting (opposite above). On the drinks table are large gold wine jars, a covered bowl for mixing wine, a bottle, a ewer and a cup on a stand. Clear wine was made from fermented rice and the emperors also enjoyed yellow wine.

Gold flask
Gold, incised
c. 1420–35
Nanjing or Beijing
h 29 cm, w 21.7 cm, d. 8.9 cm
Smithsonian American
Art Museum

Iron, bronze and tin

In the Ming dynasty, iron-smelting flourished in
Zunhua (Hebei province), Yangcheng (Shanxi
province), Foshan (Guangdong province) and Laiwu
(Shandong province). Bronze is made of copper and
tin with variable amounts of iron, lead and zinc.
Lead and zinc are extracted today from Hunan,
Anhui, Jiangxi and Yunnan. Copper deposits are
more widespread. Conditions in Ming mines were
difficult and dangerous, and consequently there
were many uprisings and riots by the miners.

Tin was mined in Southern China. Regional
princes, such as Prince Zhuang of Liang, used
model sets of tin ritual vessels for burial, as a sign
of frugality and obedience to the Ming founder, the
Hongwu emperor, who decreed that these sets
should be made of cheap and readily available
metal. Such models, made to scale, now represent
our only evidence of how many everyday items
such as lamps actually looked.

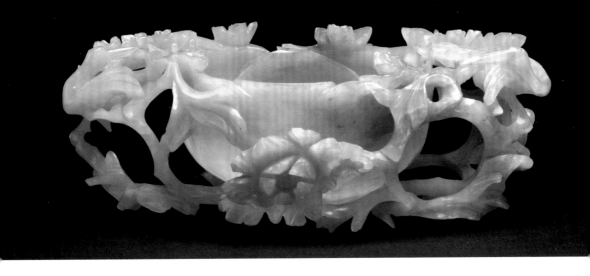

Jade

Since ancient times, jade has been associated in Chinese culture with the ability to confer immortality. In the early Ming, jade was sourced from river boulders, but from the sixteenth century onwards it was quarried from mountains, increasing the supply of jade and thus the ownership of worked jades. Early Ming princes wore belts made of carved jades imported from Hetian in modern-day Xinjiang region. Their wives had jewellery made of jade, such as hairpins and pendants. Some were simple carved jades, while others were surrounded by gold and precious gems.

Later in the Ming, jade cups were not necessarily used but symbolized conspicuous wealth. When the goods belonging to Minister Yan Song (1480–1565) were confiscated in a corruption case, records showed he owned 311 jade cups. Similarly, jade objects used for writing included wrist rests, ink paste boxes, brush rests, brush washers, brush pots and animal-shaped weights. Scholars collected and admired antique jades.

Ceramics

In the early Ming, imperial ceramics were made in Jiangxi, Zhejiang and Henan provinces. Potters in the town of Jingdezhen in Jiangxi produced blue-and-white porcelains for court commissions. The two moon-shaped flasks illustrated overleaf were made at a time when there was a real fashion for Middle Eastern forms and decoration at the Chinese court. This coincided with the move of the capital to Beijing, where collections of Egyptian and Syrian metalwork and glass perhaps remained from the period when the city was the Mongol capital. The higher quality vessels were also exported. The flask with the shortened neck (p. 51) carries a Mughal emperor's name 'Alamgir (Awrangzib) (r. 1658–1707), together with the Hijra date 1070 (1659–60). The flask may have reached the Mughal court through trade or as a diplomatic gift.

Kiln workers at Longquan in Zhejiang fired green-glazed stonewares. Artisans at the Juntai kilns in Henan made purple and lavender flower pots and thick table wares. Jingdezhen thrived and expanded as a production centre throughout the Ming, making wares for the domestic and export markets as well as for court use. Longquan continued to make heavy green wares, but by the late Ming these fell out of fashion and their quality declined after the fifteenth century when imperial patronage was withdrawn. At Dehua in Fujian province, potters made fine white porcelain vessels and figures in the sixteenth and seventeenth centuries. Scholars commissioned tea wares and items for their writing tables from the Yixing kilns in Jiangsu province, which specialized in brick-coloured unglazed stonewares.

Textiles

Ming China produced a staggering array of textiles. These were available in a range of bright colours, many with embroidered details. The imperial family wore costumes of yellow silk emblazoned with dragons (see p. 9). Silk production in the Ming dynasty was centred on the lower Yangtze valley, in towns such as Huzhou, Nanjing, Suzhou and Hangzhou, and in Sichuan, including the towns of Chengdu and Baoning (Langzhong). Silk was made for court orders, and for domestic and export markets.

The technology to weave textiles improved in the early Ming period. Textiles of extremely complicated weave and large sizes were made on new looms and some were presented as diplomatic gifts. Fine white cottons were woven in Songjiang, near modern-day Shanghai. The cloth was sometimes dyed or decorated with printed designs. Fine embroidery was produced for high-ranking officials and their families. However, few carpets and even fewer types of velvet survive from this time.

Moon flasks
Porcelain with underglaze
cobalt-blue decoration
1403–24
Jingdezhen, Jiangxi province
h 22 cm, 25 cm
British Museum

Ming *art, people and places*

Red silk robe with blue edging
1400–1600
China
h 118 cm, w 250 cm
Shandong Museum, Confucian
(Kong) Mansion Collections

Detail of silk brocade
Brocade silk and gold
1403–24
China
h 295 cm (including tassels),
w (max) 193 cm
Private Collection

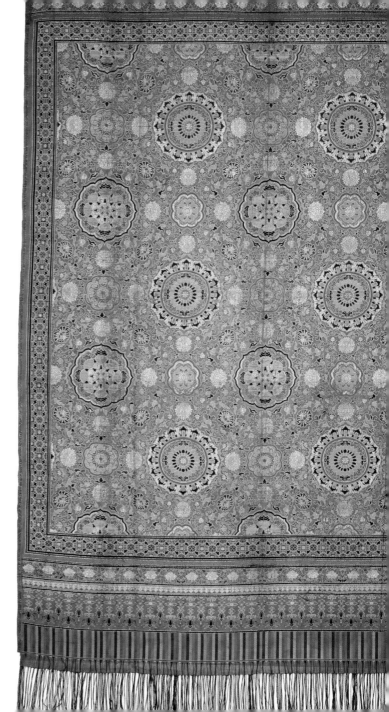

Books

Some books, such as the *Great Canon of the Yongle era* (*Yongle da dian*), were made in manuscript copies; other books were printed using carved wooden blocks. During the Ming dynasty, literacy increased dramatically among both men and women. Books were published on a vast range of subjects, including science and technology. For example, *Exploiting the Works of Nature* (*Tiangong kaiwu*), published in eighteen volumes in 1637, provides a fascinating insight into late Ming industry, including weaving, and metal and jade production. The *Compendium of Materia Medica* (*Bencao gangmu*), written by Li Shizhen over a period of twenty-six years (1552–78), was a monumental study of Chinese plants. The Ming dynasty also saw the flourishing of the novel, earlier than this form was developed in Europe. Wonderful books were written in the Ming dynasty, such as the *Romance of the Three Kingdoms* (*San guo yanyi*) by Luo Guanzhong, and *Journey to the West* (*Xi you ji*), popularly known as *Monkey*, by Wu Cheng'en. In the late Ming, women writers became more prominent.

Furniture

Ming furniture, rather like Ming ceramics, is regarded as the apogee of Chinese furniture production. It was characterized by clean lines, although these were hidden by textile coverings in everyday use in the period. An example is this horseshoe-back chair (opposite). Decorative furniture, incorporating beautiful coloured woods and bright painted designs, was also popular. The folding screen pictured overleaf was decorated with a feast at the palace of the immortal Queen Mother of the West (*Xi Wang Mu*). Such screens were used to divide room spaces both indoors and outdoors.

Bamboo and ivory carving

Amateur and professional carvers were attracted to bamboo, as they found the soft surfaces of both the root and the stem relatively easy to work. Professional carvers also made ivory tusks into figures of popular gods as well as items for a writing desk.

Horseshoe-back chair
Huali wood
1550–1650
China
h 97 cm, h of seat 50.5 cm,
l of seat 59 cm
Victoria and Albert Museum

OVERLEAF
Twelve-panelled screen
Lacquered and gilded
teak wood
c.1625–50
China
h 250.4 cm, w 587.5 cm
Victoria and Albert Museum

Domestic trade

Chinese goods were traded nationally and internationally. Livestock markets were held at strategic points such as Datong (Shanxi province) and Zhangjiakou (Hebei province) to conduct trade along the northern border. Tea, textiles, salt and iron were traded by the Chinese for horses and other livestock from northern peoples such as the Mongols. Itinerant salesmen were easily identified by their large open umbrellas and laden carts (see p. 31). Small items were suspended from every edge of the cart, attracting customers of all ages. City markets created a lively atmosphere where food, antiques and everyday items such as swords and books were purchased; street performers provided entertainment. Shops sold goods from across China, with paper money, copper coins and silver ingots changing hands.

International trade

In the early Ming period, trade was facilitated by the presentation of gifts between courts. The emperors regarded these presents as an acknowledgement of China's supremacy, but in fact it was a form of trade using tribute gifts as commodities. For example, cordial tribute relations were established with courts in the Middle East, Southeast Asia, Japan and Korea. Later in the dynasty, merchants traded goods with these countries, some of them made in specific forms or with designs particular to individual markets. Written Chinese could be understood by educated people in Japan, Korea and Vietnam, which must have assisted trade. However, pirates disrupted coastal trade in Zhejiang and Fujian.

Trade with Southeast Asia followed the earlier Yuan dynasty trade routes. A late Ming map, donated to the Bodleian Library at Oxford University in 1659 by a lawyer named John Selden (1584–1654) (see p. 62), shows the shipping routes covered by Ming merchants,

Anonymous, 'Horse with Chinese Grooms', a scene recording a tribute gift
Double-page painting, opaque pigment and silk
1400–1500
Grooms: h 39.9 cm, w 28.2 cm
Horse: h 49 cm, w 30.4 cm
Topkapi Palace Museum

RIGHT
Detail of Persian men filling up flasks with wine. Blue-and-white porcelain is on the table (far right). The paper on which this is painted was imported from China to northern Iran.
Gold decorated paper with ink with opaque colours
Paper 1400–50, manuscript completed 1468
Shamakha (Shirvan), Northern Iran
h 12 cm, w 7.5 cm
British Library

marking China, Korea, Japan, the Philippines, Indonesia, Southeast Asia and parts of India. Along these maritime routes, numerous finds of shipwreck cargoes, including vast numbers of ceramics, testify to the scale of Ming trade by sea. Overland routes through the deserts and mountains of modern western China were also used in the Ming, linking the Chinese empire with Central Asia, Iran and Iraq. Sometimes the volume of trade was interrupted by official bans.

In the 1400s and 1500s very few Chinese goods arrived in Europe and those that did were owned by the nobility. Europeans marvelled at the fineness and shiny surface of porcelain and struggled to replicate it using local materials. Europeans mounted some treasured porcelains in gold and silver, such as this pyx cup, which was used for communion bread.

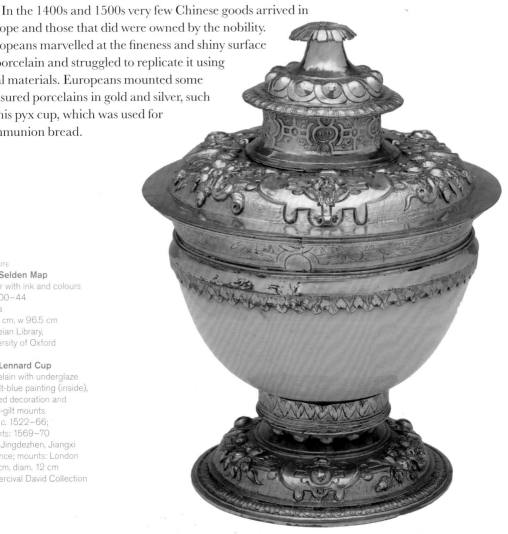

Ming *art, people and places*

In the 1600s, the Dutch and British East India companies increased the numbers of porcelains arriving within Europe and they became accessible to the middle classes. Blue-and-white porcelain can be seen displayed in this Dutch picture of *c.* 1630–5. Divers and archaeologists have recovered shipwreck cargoes from the late Ming with porcelains in distinctively European shapes, such as Dutch mustard pots, as well as large quantities of tea wares, demonstrating how quickly Chinese Ming merchants adapted their product ranges to suit different markets. Although today we have many ceramics, we have very few of the perishable goods that would have formed the bulk of the trade: tea, speciality woods, fruits and other organic products.

Anonymous, Dutch school, Enkhuizen, 'The Visit'
Oil on wood
c. 1630–5
The Netherlands
h 85.7 cm, w 117.6 cm
Museum of Art and History, Geneva

Teapot from the Hatcher shipwreck
Porcelain with underglaze cobalt-blue decoration
1640–4
Jingdezhen, Jiangxi province
h 13 cm, w 19 cm
British Museum

4

Ming tombs and their occupants

A funeral procession, from the *Great Canon of the Yongle Reign* (*Yongle da dian*)
Ink on paper, silk cover
Original edition 1403–8, this edition 1562–72
Original edition Nanjing, this edition Beijing
Book h 50.5 cm, w 30 cm
British Library

I n this section we turn our attention to a whole world beneath the ground, which often sheds an interesting light on the scant remains of society left above ground. Some of the most extraordinary Ming objects that survive today – furniture, textiles, jewellery and gold – were excavated from tombs.

In Ming China, dealing with a death comprised three distinct activities: constructing and furnishing a place of burial; holding a funeral ceremony; and mourning and preserving the memory of the deceased. Burying a person without the correct observance of these processes could create a 'hungry ghost' that would disturb the living.

Choosing a place for burial

Professional adepts chose ideal grave plots in a location facing south, with mountains behind and water in front. Intense competition for the most auspicious sites led to a growth in litigation over grave sites. The spread of printing in the Ming enabled family members to record grave sites, so as to minimize disputes. They also buried plaques explaining their legitimate right to this piece of ground. Buddhist monks and nuns were cremated, but most people were buried. Graves were often located in land given to temples on condition that monks or nuns would conduct services on behalf of the deceased. Alternatively, religious institutions could be founded specifically to ensure that a person was remembered in perpetuity. Funerals were an important opportunity to display family wealth and prestige.

The spirit way of the tomb of the Jiajing emperor's parents at Zhongxiang, Hubei, built in 1529

Imperial tombs

For more than a decade before Beijing was declared the primary capital, the Yongle emperor had planned to build the Ming imperial palace and tombs there. When his wife Empress Xu died in 1407, he did not bury her in Nanjing, which was then the primary capital, but sent officials to look for a suitable site in the Beijing area. In 1409 a site was identified that was to become the burial ground of thirteen successive Ming emperors, known today as the Ming Tombs.

The tombs were built, both above and below ground, like palaces and they were approached by a stone 'spirit way', comprising sculptures of people, such as generals and civil officials, and of animals, such as camels and horses, and of imagined or mythical creatures. A single spirit way served the entire complex. Administrative offices were set up at the imperial tombs to guard against tomb robbers and to administer sacrifices and ceremonies in memory of ancestors. Only one of the Ming tombs, belonging to the Wanli emperor (r. 1573–1620) and his wives, has been fully excavated. The buildings above ground have been repaired and reconstructed on the original site.

The Jiajing emperor provoked controversy by creating imperial tombs for his own parents in Zhongxiang, Hubei. Officials advised the new emperor to accept the previous Zhengde emperor as his own father and to leave his real parents in their more modest tombs. His defiant actions threatened the idea of a single unbroken imperial line back to the Ming founder.

The underground tomb of Zhu Yuelian, the Prince of Shu (died 1409)

Princely tombs

Princely tombs were also constructed like model palaces above and below ground. Inside, they were furnished with real and replica goods. Made-to-scale model furniture has been excavated from the tomb of Zhu Tan (1370–1389), Prince of Lu. Such furniture is extremely rare in the early Ming period, but is more common in later Ming tombs of the sixteenth and seventeenth centuries. From these models we can reconstruct an idea of the prince's sleeping quarters, his utensils for personal ablutions and dining equipment. Details of the bed (see overleaf) are executed perfectly, such as the rolled bamboo mat for summertime coolness, the soft silk pillow and the thick padded silk mattress. Practical equipment included a wash basin set on a stand and a towel rack with a white fine-cotton towel. The chest has bronze fittings, and traces of its painted lacquer and gold decoration remain. The tomb also included different varieties of wooden tables and chairs, as well as storehouses for grain and poultry, and woven baskets for storage of other goods.

Other tombs

Very little is known of the lives of the vast majority of the 85 million people who lived in Ming China. They mostly worked on the land, growing food for daily life and cash crops such as tea, cotton and rice. Ordinary people were buried simply and with few tomb goods. Few commoners' graves have been excavated. In Ming China, social distinctions were maintained for eternity and it was important that the spirit world knew all about the past history and status of the deceased. Their careers continued beyond the grave.

Tomb models

Tomb models of domestic houses provide an insight into how people lived. Some feature living quarters, storerooms, ornamental gates and a protective screen to prevent ghosts entering the complex. The space in between the buildings indicated courtyards. As few wooden buildings from the Ming era survive today, these provide a fascinating insight into Ming architecture. Tomb models were not present in all Ming burials. Their quantity, quality and subject matter varied greatly from burial to burial. Models were made using various materials; examples in earthenware, stone and metals such as tin have been found.

Opening up some tombs has revealed undisturbed processions of servants engaged in a range of duties, like dolls in a toy house. Many of the figures are musicians playing rousing ritual music on instruments such as drums and trumpets rather than on instruments of entertainment, such as lutes or zithers, which had been popular in earlier burials. There are few model animals other than horses; again, this contrasts with earlier burials. Model food has also been discovered, which helps us to understand people's diet.

Tomb model of a female
servant
Glazed earthenware
c. 1550–1600
North China
h 21 cm
British Museum

OPPOSITE ABOVE
Tomb model bed belonging to
Zhu Tan, Prince Huang of Lu
(1370–1389)
Wood, silk, bamboo and lacquer
c. 1389
Shandong province
h 36.4 cm, w 19.5cm, l 38.5cm
Shandong Museum

OPPOSITE BELOW
A group of model food
Glazed earthenware
c.1450–1600
North China
h 3 cm, w (max) 12.8 cm
British Museum

Real goods in tombs

Middle-class merchants, doctors and scholars were buried with the tools of their trades. Their wives were interred with goods appropriate to their rank in a hierarchical society. Archaeologists have uncovered the Ming tomb of a doctor, Xia Shudu (1348–1411), in which they discovered a range of medical equipment including pots for storing and administering medicines, toothbrushes, tweezers and scissors. Swords and military equipment were interred in the tombs of military men: General Mu Ying's (1345–1392) tomb included his sword and scabbard. Paintings and antiques have been discovered in the burial places of scholars and collectors, as well as of members of the increasingly rich merchant class.

Luxury goods were also included in burials. Raw materials such as bolts of cloth may have been intended to be finished in the afterlife or used as currency. Descendants buried their relatives dressed in their best robes and included other fine silk costumes as spare clothes. This pair of fine embroidered shoes was one of three pairs included in the tomb of Mrs Zhou, wife of a scholar of middling rank, who was buried in Wuxi, Jiangsu in 1403–24. Her feet were bound to make them smaller, but not as tiny as the women of the subsequent Qing dynasty.

A pair of women's shoes belonging to Mrs Zhou
Embroidered silk
c. 1403–24
Jiangsu province
l 22.5 cm
China National Silk Museum, Hangzhou, excavated in 2002 from a tomb on the east side of the Tai Lake, Wuxi, Jiangsu

Rank badge for a sixth-rank civil official showing a pair of egrets. Rank badges with different animal and bird designs were worn by all officials, as we can see in the portraits overleaf.
Silk tapestry *kesi* and metal-wrapped threads
*c.*1500 – 1600
China
h 32 cm, w 35 cm
Victoria and Albert Museum

Preserving the memory of the dead

Before photography, commissioning paintings or sculptures of individuals was the only effective way of recording and remembering their likenesses. Memorial portraits played an important role in rituals and services to revere the deceased, both within families and more widely in lineages, for priests and the imperial family. The main method of representing the individuals in and of the Ming is with the full figure shown, seated on a textile draped chair, within a minimally defined interior space. The lack of background features forced the viewers to focus on the subject's face. Portraits were hung on special occasions, including at New Year, to involve the ancestor in family celebrations. Food offerings were made in front of the hanging scroll images.

Ancestors whose likenesses were not captured at the time were later depicted in costume appropriate to their era. Artists also painted the face with great detail and one imagines with great fidelity to the subject. However, to enhance the status of the living, they were painted wearing costumes, sometimes of high ranking officials. In the Ming-style portrait illustrated overleaf, a grey-haired woman, perhaps sixty years old, is shown wearing a headdress of kingfisher feathers and pearls, and red silk robes with an embroidered rank badge. In the accompanying painting, a male relative is dressed as a Ming official.

Portrait of an unknown woman with Ming kingfisher feather headdress
Hanging scroll ink and colours on silk
c.1600–44,
or later 1700–1800
China
Image: h 119.5 cm, w 77.5 cm
Mount: h 218.5 cm,
w 83.5 cm
British Museum

Portrait of an unknown man with Ming official's hat and robe
Hanging scroll ink and colours on silk
c.1600–44,
or later 1700–1800
China
Image: h 127 cm, w 80.5 cm
Mount: h 255 cm, w 96.5 cm
British Museum

5

Religious sites and their communities

A ssimilating diverse aspects of different religious traditions and systems of belief, and then applying them to distinct parts of daily life, is characteristic of most Chinese history but is particularly marked in the early Ming (1400–1450). The complex spiritual and religious landscape included various sects of Buddhism and Daoism, with their dedicated buildings, religious specialists and texts, and numerous cults. Significant Muslim communities thrived, as well as residual Jewish ones. Later in the 1500s, European Jesuits arrived in Ming China and Christianity began to be included in this religious mix.

Official religion

Chinese belief held that the emperor enjoyed Heaven's blessing. At their courts, the Ming emperor and princes conducted services with sacrifices and prayers to ancestors, to Heaven, to Earth and to a pantheon of officially recognized gods and goddesses on behalf of all the people in the Ming empire. Each of these services required specific vessels, costumes, movements and words. Correct performances were essential to bring prosperity and peace to the empire, and to maintain them.

The Bureau of Sacrifices of the Ministry of Rites and the Court of Imperial Sacrifices were responsible for organizing these services. The Temple of Spirit Music supplied dancers and musicians. The Directorate of Astronomy ensured auspicious timing for the rituals. The Ministry of Works built the altars and temples, liaising with the Ministry of Rites on their construction and the Ministry of Revenue on their financing. Many different kinds of official service were conducted. Arguably the most important were those to the celestial souls of the imperial ancestors. Private services were held at the Ancestral Temple (Tai Miao) outside the city walls, in the domestic chapel within the palace, the Palace of Honouring the Ancestors (Feng Xian dian), and at the Ming Tombs.

Buddhism

From the early Ming, the imperial family were directly involved in the religious life of their subjects. A very close relationship existed between the imperial court and Buddhist monastic communities. The Hongwu emperor, founder of the Ming dynasty, had been a monk himself between the ages of about seventeen and twenty-four. The Yongle emperor wrote books of hymns, and a tome describing historical monks, *Biographies of supernatural monks*.

Buddhism was lavishly patronized by the court and its promotion in the early Ming led to new models of religious practice, as well as new forms of image, which have lasted until the present day. Imperial courts of the Yongle and Xuande emperors followed Yuan precedent and relied on Himalayan Buddhism to create a visual vocabulary for the representation of Buddhist deities. Artisans from Tibet and Nepal remained in Beijing after the fall of the Yuan and went on to serve in the imperial workshops. Exchanges of sculptures between the Ming court and Tibetan hierarchs were frequent.

Daoism

Although Buddhism originated in India, Daoism developed in China. By the Ming dynasty both religions had interacted for centuries. By the early fifteenth century, Daoism had long been seen as an organized religion, with official buildings, priests, ritual practice and texts. Daoist deities were often depicted alongside gods from a broad popular pantheon. The *Scripture of the Jade Pivot* (see overleaf) is a woodblock-printed Daoist scripture book that details one of the most important liturgical aspects of the religion – harnessing nature through control of thunder and rain. The scene illustrated shows musicians performing in front of a temple. The manuscript combines religious iconography, the supernatural and everyday life (images of childbirth, funerals, umbrellas, carpenters, wheelbarrows and butchery). These are shown alongside rains of flowers and magical meetings of deities. In the scenes of daily life, the idea is that the thunder god will protect people in

The Celestial Worthy
of Primordial Being
Stoneware with
polychrome glazes
1488–1644
Possibly Shanxi province
h123.3 cm, w 78 cm,
d 55 cm
British Museum,

Mount Wudang, Hubei province

OPPOSITE
Scripture of the Jade Pivot
(Yushu jing)
Woodblock-printed, ink on paper
1403–24
h 34 cm, w 12 cm (each folding page)
The British Library

Zhenwu on Mount Wudang
Bronze with traces of paint
and lacquer
1522–66
Hubei province
h 117 cm
British Museum

every situation. The scripture will help anyone who recites it in times of ill fortune or poor health. The pronunciation of difficult characters is written down to help its oral delivery.

The Celestial Masters managed Daoist official lineages across China and were called upon by the Ming emperors to perform rituals and court music. Rituals could include ceremonies to summon good weather and to control storms, or even exorcism rituals. The Celestial Master Zhang Yuchu (1361–1410) received an imperial commission from the Yongle emperor in 1406 to gather texts for the official canon of Daoism, the *Daozang*, which was an overview of current Daoist texts and practices. This was completed in the Zhengtong emperor's reign (1436–1449).

From 1412 onwards, the Yongle emperor commissioned a major series of temples and shrines to be built on the summits of the highest peaks in the Mount Wudang area of Hubei province, in honour of Zhenwu, the god of War and protector of the Ming dynasty. The Jiajing emperor was born in Hubei and founded a new line of Ming emperors in 1522. He extensively refurbished these temples on Mount Wudang, commissioning numerous new sculptures of Zhenwu.

Islam

A significant minority of Muslims lived in China in the early Ming and were often given the Chinese surname Ma. Some made the pilgrimage to Mecca, evidenced by the name 'Hajji' – a title added after the journey had been made. In 1407 the Yongle emperor officially issued an edict protecting Muslim clerics within the Ming empire, written in classical Chinese, Persian and Mongolian. Muslims were employed at the imperial court in the Bureau of Translators, as eunuchs within the palace, as part of the army, and as astronomers and mathematicians. Ambassadors from the Middle East also made voyages to the Ming Court. The family of Zheng He (1371–1433), the famous eunuch admiral who served both the Yongle and Xuande emperors, was Muslim. Zheng He renovated Jingjue mosque in Nanjing, but he also repaired Buddhist and Daoist temples. Mosques were built in many cities across China in the early Ming.

A page from *The Lineage of Buddhas* showing a couple praying at a Buddhist shrine (detail)
Woodblock-printed, ink on paper
China
c. 1423
Each leaf: h 36.6 cm, w 23.8 cm
Muban Foundation

Clerics

Buddhist clerics played important roles at Ming courts. Literate monks published popular religious books that circulated widely, spreading knowledge of religious texts and historical tales related to worship. Baocheng (active 1425), a monk from Ningbo, described the detailed events leading up to the birth of the Buddha, his life, and the early history of the Buddhist movement with 400 illustrations. As an example of woodblock printing for ordinary Buddhist devotees, *The Lineage of Buddha*s may be cruder than books produced at court. It has rougher designs and less regular characters, but it is valuable evidence of the beliefs of many people in the early Ming.

Monks were also featured in popular novels such as the *Journey to the West* (also called *Monkey*), attributed to Wu Cheng'en (about 1500–1582). This popular Ming novel loosely bases its story on the adventures of a famous historical monk. The novel was so popular that images from it were taken as inspiration for roof ornaments, such as this ridge tile in the forn of a standing monk.

Standing monk ridge tile
Stoneware with glazes
c. 1490–1620
Shanxi province
h 40.5 cm, l 17 cm, d 12 cm
British Museum

Temple of Attained
Wisdom (Zhihua si),
Beijing

Buildings

In the Ming period, monasteries, nunneries, temples and mosques were
built across China. Monastic communities were substantial. By the mid
1450s, in Beijing alone there were more than one thousand Buddhist
monasteries. Both imperial and regional court patronage was important to
this Ming construction boom and to the successful functioning of the
buildings as centres for prayer and study. The Yongle emperor commissioned
the 'Great Monastery of Filial Gratitude' (Da Baoensi) in Nanjing, with its
nine-storey porcelain pagoda. High-ranking eunuchs also patronized
religious institutions. Two Ming temples in Beijing still survive, and both
were supported by eunuch patronage – the 'Temple of the Sea of the Law'
(Fahai si) and the 'Temple of Attained Wisdom' (Zhihua si).

Meditational diagram
Ink and colours on silk
Dated 1479
Beijing, acquired from the
'Temple of Great and Mighty
Benevolence that Protects
the Dynasty') (*Da Long shan
hu guo si*)
h 151 cm, l99.1 cm
Victoria and Albert Museum

    Monasteries also served as hostels for travellers from within China and
from abroad. This meditational diagram was acquired from a temple in the
north-west of Beijing, 'Temple of Great and Mighty Benevolence that
Protects the Dynasty' (*Da Long shan hu guo si*), which regularly housed visiting
monks in the Ming dyansty.

As well as erecting new buildings, the courts also regularly paid for repairs to existing buildings, which was regarded as an act of merit. Parts of the Ming army were employed to oversee ambitious restoration projects and court artists were deployed to paint temple wall murals.

Between 1490 and 1600, there was a real building boom in China patronized by the middle classes. The roof tile below, modelled in the form of a demon, was made to ornament the top ridge of a non-imperial building.

Texts

The Ming court published lavish and complete orthodox versions of Buddhist and Daoist texts. Some were printed for use within the imperial court but others were made to be presented to monasteries and temples across China. Copies were then made outside the courts as an act of piety and imperial association, and disseminated further. Most of these texts were printed using carved woodblocks for both the illustrations and the text. Imperially sponsored printing was overseen by eunuchs working in the Directorate of Ceremonial, who insured the very high quality of the preparation and cutting of the woodblocks for printing.

Ridge tile
Stoneware with glazes
1490–1620
Probably Shanxi province
h 37 cm, l 25 cm
British Museum

Services

Buddhist clergy were required to perform religious ceremonies. Some famous religious figures travelled thousands of miles to conduct services at the emperor's behest. For example, an entourage of Buddhist priests from Tibet spent three years crossing China to reach Nanjing to conduct a memorial service for the Yongle emperor's parents. Some of the miraculous events that occurred as a result of these rituals are recorded in early fifteenth century paintings with texts in many languages, suggesting a multi-cultural audience for some imperial rituals. Private ceremonies were also performed by the emperor and members of the court. Daoist priests were employed to stage important rituals too.

Detail from the 'Miracles of Nanjing' showing monks
Ink and colours on paper
1403–1424
Nanjing
l 4968 cm
Tibet Museum

FOLLOWING PAGES
Detail from the 'Miracles of Nanjing' showing coloured clouds and multiple multi-coloured rainbows appearing over Nanjing
Ink and colours on paper
1403–1424
Nanjing
l 4968 cm
Tibet Museum

Acknowledgements

First and foremost I would like to record my thanks to Professor Craig Clunas, who has been a great inspiration throughout our five year joint project. Dr Luk Yu-ping has worked so hard to support the project and has enriched it at every point along the way. There have been many volunteers to thank but particular gratitude goes to Malcolm McNeil, Jean Martin and Keith Southall, who have all helped in different ways. With Jan Stuart and all my colleagues in the Asia department at the British Museum I have received a very special kind of support – each contributing their individual and collective expertise. Colleagues at the British Library, V&A, SOAS and Bodleian Library are all thanked for their kindness. Especial thanks for materials to Roderick Whitfield, Christer von der Berg, Christopher Bruckner, Alison Hardie, Timothy Brook, David Robinson and Marsha Haufler. For reading the text on behalf of the non-specialist audience, I would like to thank Martin Keady. For producing this book with good humour, unending gratitude to Coralie Hepburn, Axelle Russo, Kate Oliver and Raymonde Watkins. For the British Museum photography, many thanks are due to John Williams and Kevin Lovelock. Finally I would also like to thank all my colleagues in China who have helped me in so many ways and the main exhibition teams in particular.

Large blue-and-white porcelain flask modelled on a Middle Eastern form
Painted with underglaze blue decoration
Xuande mark and period, 1426–1435
Jingdezhen
h 51 cm, diam 23.5 cm
British Museum

Bibliography

Barnhart, Richard M., with essays by Mary Ann Rogers, Richard Stanley-Baker, *Painters of the Great Ming: The Imperial Court and the Zhe School*, Dallas, 1993.

Brinker, Helmut and Albert Lutz, *Chinese Cloisonné: The Pierre Uldry Collection*, Asia Society, New York, 1989.

Brook, Timothy, *Praying for Power: Buddhism and the Formation of Gentry Society in late-Ming China*, Cambridge MA and London, 1993.

Brook, Timothy, *The Confusions of Pleasure: Commerce and Culture in Ming China*, Berkeley, 1998.

Brook, Timothy, *The Troubled Empire: China in the Yuan and Ming Dynasties*, Cambridge, MA, and London, 2010.

Brown, Roxanna, *The Ming Gap and Shipwreck Ceramics in Southeast Asia: Towards a Chronology of Thai Trade Ware*, Bangkok, 2009.

Cahill, James, *The Distant Mountains: Chinese Painting of the Late Ming Dynasty 1570–1644*, New York and Tokyo, 1982.

Chia Lin Sien and Sally K. Church (eds), *Zheng He and the Afro-Asian World*, Melaka 2012.

Craig Clunas, *Superfluous Things: Material Culture and Social Status in Early Modern China*, Honolulu, 2004.

Clunas, Craig, *Empire of Great Brightness: Visual and Material Cultures of Ming China, 1368–1644*, London, 2007.

Clunas, Craig, *Screen of Kings: Royal Art and Power in Ming China*, London, 2013.

Clunas, Craig and Harrison-Hall, Jessica (eds), *Ming: 50 years that changed China*, London, 2014.

Dreyer, Edward L., *Early Ming China*, Stanford, 1982.

Dreyer, Edward L., *Zheng He, China and the Oceans in the Early Ming Dynasty, 1405–1433*, New York, 2007.

Eng Sunchuan Clarence, 'The use of ceramic in Chinese late imperial architecture', PhD thesis, SOAS, University of London, 2008.

Farmer, Edward L., *Early Ming Government: The Evolution of Dual Capitals*, Cambridge, MA, 1976.

Giuffrida, Noelle, 'Representing the Daoist god Zhenwu, the Perfected Warrior, in late imperial China', PhD thesis, University of Kansas, 2008.

Gugong bowuyuan 故宮博物院 (Palace Museum, Beijing), *Junci yaji: Gugong bowuyuan zhencang ji chutu junyao ciqi huicui* 鈞瓷雅集: 故宮博物院珍藏及出土鈞窯瓷器薈萃 (*Selection of Jun Ware – The Palace Museum's Collection and Archaeological Excavation*), Beijing, 2013.

Harrison-Hall, Jessica, *Ming Ceramics – A Catalogue of the Late Yuan and Ming Ceramics in the British Museum*, London, 2001.

Hay, Jonathan, *Sensuous Surfaces: The Decorative Object in Early Modern China*, London, 2009.

Höllmann, Thomas O. (trans. Karen Margolis), *The Land of the Five Flavors: A Cultural History of Chinese Cuisine*, New York, 2013.

Hong Kong Museum of Art, *Heavens' Embroidered Cloths: One Thousand Years of Chinese Textiles*, exh. cat. Hong Kong, 1995.

Hubeisheng bowuguan 湖北省博物館 (Hubei Provincial Museum), *Liangzhuang wangmu: Zheng He shidai de guibao* 梁莊王墓：鄭和時代的瑰寶 (*The Tomb of Prince Liangzhuang: Treasure of the Era of Zheng He*), Beijing, 2007.

Jiang Cheng'an and Zheng Wenlei (eds), *Precious Deposits: Historical Relics of Tibet, China, vol. 3*, Beijing, 2000.

Karmay, Heather, *Early Sino-Tibetan Art*, Warminster, 1975.

Kerr, Rose, *Later Chinese Bronzes*, London, 1990.

Kerr, Rose and Rosemary, Scott, *Ceramic Evolution in the Middle Ming Period : Hongzhi to Wanli (1488–1620)*, London, 1994.

Krahl, Regina, *Chinese Ceramics in the Topkapi Saray Museum Istanbul, vols 1–3*, London, 1986.

Lam, Joseph S.C., *State Sacrifices and Music in Ming China: Orthodoxy, Creativity, and Expressiveness*, New York, 1998.

Lam, Peter (ed.), *Layered Beauty: The Baoyizhai Collection of Chinese Lacquer*, Hong Kong, 2010.

Lee King-tse and Hu Shih-chang, 'Carved lacquer of the Hongwu period', *Oriental Art*, vol. 47, no. 1, 2001, pp. 10–20.

Li Baoping, 'Numbered Jun wares: controversies and new kiln site discoveries', *Transactions of the Oriental Ceramic Society*, vol. 71 no. 1, 2008, pp. 65–77.

Li He and Michael Knight (eds), *Power and Glory: Court Arts of China's Ming Dynasty*, exh. cat., San Francisco, 2008.

Liscomb, Kathlyn, 'Foregrounding the symbiosis of power: a rhetorical strategy in some Chinese commemorative art', *Art History*, vol. 25, no. 2, 2002, pp. 135–61.

Little, Stephen with Shawn Eichman, *Taoism and the Arts of China*, Chicago, 2000.

Luk Yu-ping, *The Empress and the Celestial Masters: A Study into the Ordination Scroll of Empress Zhang (1493)*, forthcoming.

Mote, Frederick W. and Denis C. Twitchett (eds), *The Cambridge History of China: Volume 7, The Ming Dynasty, 1368–1644, Part 1*, Cambridge, 1988.

Naquin, Susan, *Peking: Temples and City Life, 1400–1900*, Berkeley, Los Angeles and London, 2000.

Paludan, Ann, *The Imperial Ming Tombs*, New Haven and Hong Kong, 1981.

Pierson, Stacey, *From Object to Concept – Global Consumption and the Transformation of Ming Porcelain*, Hong Kong, 2013.

Quette, Beatrice (ed.), *Cloisonné: Chinese Enamels from the Yuan, Ming and Qing Dynasties*, New York, Paris, New Haven and London, 2012.

Rawson, Jessica and Carol Michaelson, *Chinese Jade: From the Neolithic to the Qing*, London, 1995.

Robinson, David M., *Bandits, Eunuchs, and the Son of Heaven: Rebellion and the Economy of Violence in Mid-Ming China*, Honolulu, 2001.

Robinson, David M. (ed.), *Culture, Courtiers, and Competition: The Ming Court (1368–1644)*, Cambridge, MA, 2008.

Robinson, David M., *Martial Spectacles of the Ming Court*, Cambridge, MA, and London, 2013.

Rossabi, Morris, *China and Inner Asia: From 1368 to the Present Day*, New York, 1975.

Schaefer, Dagmar and Dieter Kuhn, *Weaving an Economic Pattern in Ming Times (1368–1644)*, Heidelberg, 2002.

Schneewind, Sarah, *A Tale of Two Melons: Emperor and Subject in Ming China*, Indianapolis, 2006.

Sen, Tansen, *Buddhism, Diplomacy, and Trade: The Realignment of Sino-Indian Relations, 600–1400*, Honolulu, 2003.

Soullière, Ellen Felicia, 'Palace women in the Ming dynasty: 1368–1644', PhD thesis, Princeton University, 1987.

Ströber, Eva, *Ming: Porcelain for a Globalised Trade*, Stuttgart, 2013.

Stuart, Jan and Evelyn S. Rawski, *Worshipping the Ancestors: Chinese Commemorative Portraits*, Washington DC, 2001.

Sung Hou Mei, *Decoded Messages: The Symbolic Language of Chinese Animal Painting*, New Haven, 2010.

Tsai Shih-shan Henry, *The Eunuchs in the Ming Dynasty*, New York, 1996.

Tsai Shih-Shan Henry, *Perpetual Happiness – The Ming Emperor Yongle*, Seattle and London, 2001.

Twitchett, Denis C. and Frederick W. Mote (eds), *The Cambridge History of China: Volume 8, The Ming Dynasty, 1368–1644, Part 2*, Cambridge, 1998.

Vainker, Shelagh, *Chinese Silk: A Cultural History*, London, 2004.

Wade, Geoff and Sun Liachen (eds), *Southeast Asia in the Fifteenth Century: The China Factor*, Singapore, 2010

Wang Cheng-hua, 'Material culture and emperorship: the shaping of imperial roles at the Court of Xuanzong (r. 1426–35)', PhD thesis, Yale University, 1998.

Wang, Helen, 'Money in the Ming dynasty', *Orientations*, Sept 2014.

Wang, Richard G., *The Ming Prince and Daoism: Institutional Patronage of an Elite*, Oxford, 2012.

Watt, James C.Y. and Barbara Brennan Ford, *East Asian Lacquer: The Florence and Herbert Irving Collection*, New York, 1991.

Watt, James C.Y. and Wen Fong, *Possessing the Past: Treasures from the National Palace Museum, Taipei*, New York, exh. cat., 1996.

Watt, James C.Y. and Anne E. Wardwell, *When Silk Was Gold: Central Asian and Chinese Textiles in The Cleveland and Metropolitan Museums of Art*, exh. cat., New York, 1997.

Watt, James C.Y. and Denise Patry Leidy, *Defining Yongle: Imperial Art in Early Fifteenth-Century China*, New York, 2005.

Weidner, Marsha (ed.), *Latter Days of the Law: Images of Chinese Buddhism 850–1850*, exh. cat., Honolulu, 1994.

Weidner, Marsha (ed.), *Cultural Intersections in Later Chinese Buddhism*, Honolulu, 2001

Whitfield, Roderick, 'The Lioness Painting' in Sotheby's Hong Kong, Friday 8 April 2011, sale catalogue.

Wilson, Ming and Ian Thomas, *Chinese Jades*, London, 2004.

Wilson, Verity, *Chinese Textiles*, London, 2005.

Wood, Nigel, *Chinese Glazes: Their Origins, Chemistry and Recreation*, London and Philadelphia, 1999.

Wu Hung (ed.), *Reinventing the Past: Antiquarianism in Chinese Art and Visual Culture*, Chicago, 2010.

Yang Xiaoneng, 'Archaeological perspectives on the princely burials of Ming dynasty enfeoffments', *Ming Studies*, vol. 65, 2012, pp. 93–118.

Zhao Feng, *Treasures in Silk: An Illustrated History of Chinese Textiles*, Hangzhou, 1999.

Zhang Hongxing (ed), *Masterpieces of Chinese Painting 700–1900*, London, 2013.

Illustration credits

Images of objects from the British Museum and Sir Percival David collections are © The Trustees of the British Museum, courtesy of the Department of Photography and Imaging. Further information about objects in the collection of the British Museum can be found on the Museum's website at britishmuseum.org.

p. 64	Musée d'art et d'histoire, ville de Genève BASZ 0005
p. 65	British Museum 1984,0303.3
p. 67	© the British Library Board, BL OR11758
p. 68	Shutterstock (photo beibaoke)
p. 69	Photograph courtesy of Sichuan Museum
p. 70	British Museum, purchased with the help of public subscription from the George Eumorfopoulos collection, 1937,0716.112
p. 71	(above) Shandong Museum
p. 71	(below) British Museum, given by Mrs A. Chester Beatty, 1927,12143.1-10
p. 72	China National Silk Museum, Hangzhou
p. 73	Victoria and Albert Museum, London
p. 74	British Museum, donated by Beatrice Bateson, 1926,0410,0.14, Ch.Ptg.Add.45
p. 75	British Museum, donated by Beatrice Bateson, 1926,0410,0.13, Ch.Ptg.Add.44
p. 77	British Museum 1908,0410.4
p. 79	British Museum, given by Harvey Hadden, 1930,0719.62
p. 80	© the British Library Board ORB 99/161
p. 81	(left) © Getty Images (photo Karl Johaentges)
p. 81	(right) British Museum 1990,1219.1
p. 82	The Muban Foundation Collection, no. 213
p. 83	British Museum 1937,0716.109
p. 84	Photograph courtesy of the Zhi Hua Temple
p. 85	Victoria and Albert Museum, London E.61-1911
p. 86	British Museum, bequeathed by F.E. Colthurst, 1946,0715.13
p. 87	Tibet Museum, Lhasa
pp. 88–9	Tibet Museum, Lhasa
p. 90	British Museum, donated by Sir John Addis, 1975,1028.19
p. 96	British Museum (artwork Paul Goodhead)

SIBERIA

MONGOLIA

ASIA

HEILONGJIANG

Amur

Songhua

Tyr

Hami

GOBI DESERT

THE STEPPE

LIAONING

Tumu Fort

Juyong Pass

Liaodong Peninsula

NORTH KOREA

Samarkand

XINJIANG AUTONOMOUS REGION
(XINJIANG UYGUR ZIZHIQU)

Xuanfu

Datong

Mount Wutai ▲

Beijing

Dalian

Seoul

SOUTH KOREA

AFGHANISTAN

QINGHAI

Yellow River

Taiyuan

SHANDONG

Jeju Island

JAPAN

CHINA

Xi'an

Kaifeng

Grand Canal

Nanjing

TIBET AUTONOMOUS REGION
(XIZANG ZIZHIQU)

HIMALAYAS

Mount Wudang ▲

Mount Zhong ▲

Suzhou

Liujiagang

Hangzhou

Shanghai

PAKISTAN

NEPAL

New Delhi

SICHUAN

HUBEI

Jingdezhen

Yangtze

YUNNAN

Taihe County

Changle

Okinawa

Ryūkyū Islands

PACIFIC OCEAN

GUJARAT

WEST BENGAL

BANGLA-DESH

Chittagong

MYANMAR (BURMA)

LAOS

Red River Delta

Nanning

Quanzhou

Xiamen

INDIA

Kozhikode (Calicut)

Cochin

Quilon

SRI LANKA

Galle

Andaman Islands

THAILAND

Ayutthaya

CAMBODIA

VIETNAM

Qui Nhon

PHILIPPINES

Nicobar Islands

Strait of Malacca

Kelantan

Banda Aceh

Semudera

Sumatra

MALAYSIA

Pahang

Malacca

BRUNEI

Sulu

Borneo

INDONESIA

Palembang

INDIAN OCEAN

Java

Surabaya

N

Zheng He's main route

Subsidiary route

Locations mentioned in the book

Istanbul

0   500   1000 miles

0   500   1000   1500 kilometres